BECOMING THE HARVEST

Caitlin Press Inc.
3375 Ponderosa Way
Qualicum Beach, BC V9K 2J8
www.caitlinpress.com

Text and cover design by Vici Johnstone
Cover artwork and illustrations "Dryas octopetala" by Julya Hajnoczky
Printed in Canada

Caitlin Press Inc. acknowledges financial support from the Government of Canada and the Canada Council for the Arts, and the Province of British Columbia through the British Columbia Arts Council and the Book Publisher's Tax Credit.

Library and Archives Canada Cataloguing in Publication
Title: Becoming the harvest / Pauline Le Bel.

Names: Le Bel, Pauline, 1943- author.
Identifiers: Canadiana 20240381742 | ISBN 9781773861562 (softcover)
Subjects: LCGFT: Poetry.

Classification: LCC PS8573.E183 B43 2024 | DDC C811/.54—dc23

Becoming the Harvest

Pauline Le Bel

Caitlin Press 2024

In loving memory of my sister Suzanne

Contents

Becoming the Harvest

On a grassy field glistening with dew
the doe chose to give in to gravity.

A frequent guest.
One I fed greens and carrots
whenever the ground
was snow shrouded.

I discovered her one morning
quiet, composed,
her legs extended,
her neck stretched in repose.

For her, dying was as natural as living.
As natural as lying down.

Can it really be this simple?
Will my animal body know what to do?

When my time comes, will I sing
lay me down, lay me down under the apple tree?

Teachings of the Chinese Lantern in My Garden

In spring, youthful heart-shaped leaves flaunt tiny white flowers.

In summer, the flowers transform into green pods.

In autumn, the pods dress themselves
outrageously in jack-o-lantern orange.

At the end of its life,
the lantern, thin, translucent,
like the chiffon of my old hands,
shelters a bright red berry,

seed for the next generation.

Blooming

Earth is four billion years old
and still beguiling us with flowers,
a project she began in her dotage.

Who knows what deep inside me
is still waiting to bloom.

Bowing

After surviving
another winter snow
the cedar bows
towards the ground,
like my aging back
greeting the morning
with gratitude.

Good Company

If we are known by the company we keep
I would be known as apple tree,
I would be known as fig.

I would be known as Golden-crowned Kinglet,
Savannah Sparrow, Western Tanager,
as virus, bacteria, mitochondria,
mountain air, lake water, sea foam.

I would be known as treble clef,
major fourth, minor fifth,
bel canto, blues and boogie woogie,
salsa, swing and soupy shuffle.

One day I will be known as wind,
soil, sand, sky, cumulus cloud.
I will be known as ancestor.

The Harpy

Ah, yes, there she is waiting for me,
head and chest of a woman,
wings and talons of a bird of prey
shrieking in that liminal space between
what I was and what I am not yet,
calling to me from the Greek myth:

Look in the mirror, you have
wings, you are free, look
at yourself you have
claws to grasp the truth,
breasts to succor the needy,
a head to navigate your way.

Wings flutter at my back.
My breasts fill with honey.
My mind swells with possibility.

The Greeks, afraid of old women.
Rightly so.

At the Salon

Good bones, Irene declares
are everything.

You've got 'em, she insists.
You'll never have to worry about turkey neck.

Well, turkey neck has never been
one of my major concerns.

But now I worry about turkeys.
They must not have good bones.

Sauerkraut

In my dotage, I've become a bit of an expert
brewing up plentiful jars of sauerkraut,
fermented carrots, beets and garlic,
offering my friends the gift of microbes.

A bit surprising since my ancestors
were more inclined to ferment wine and cheese.

Shred the cabbage, add flavourings:
apple, carrot, fennel, ginger, garlic.
Knead the cabbage with salt
until the liquids are drawn out.

Wait a few weeks and the bubbles
convert carbohydrates into lactic acid,
making the veggies more digestible,
nutritious and probiotic.

An alchemical process much like aging.
A slow, gentle, unstoppable force for change.

God's Waiting Room

That's what my neighbour, Ed, called this place
when I moved in sixteen years ago.

A senior's co-op.
One-storey row houses.
Light blue siding with cedar trim.

A common building with a lounge,
sofas adorned with lacy antimacassars.
An activity room with a piano
and exercise bikes, some of which actually work.

A community garden with raised beds
for aging knees and backs.
A courtyard with Adirondack chairs
for afternoon gossip.

Old people on the Board of Directors.
Old people on the Maintenance Committee.
Old people spying on neighbours through venetian blinds.

Old people pruning apple trees
and falling off ladders as they watch
turkey vultures circle overhead.

Keeping ourselves busy down here
on standby at heaven's door.

A Handful of Soil

I scoop up a handful of soil from my garden
and inhale the sweet smell of death:
dead roots, leaves, worms, bugs, microbes.

I dip my trowel into the moist earth,
place the snap pea seeds into the ground.
I almost forget to say thank you.

Morning Fog

morning fog
stalks the bay
veils the sky
paints the sea white

I retreat
under feathers
and flannel

ferry blast
the only proof
of life
beyond my bed

Ripe

You can't rush ripe. You can't wish ripe.
You can't arm twist, flatter, beguile, butter up
or set a timer for ripe.

Ripe happens in its own sweet time.
It's a matter of patience.

Place the yellow mango
in the wooden fruit bowl. And wait.

I mean *wait*. Slice it before its time
and your mouth will miss the show.

Observe the mango daily.
Wait until the colour deepens
until the fruit welcomes the soft cup of your hand,
until the scent of a summer breeze
fills your imagination and you remember
skinny dipping in the phosphorescent sea.

Now the mango will give you
everything a mango was born to do.

Much the same with an old woman.

You must wait until her eyes crease at the sides
from looking deep into your eyes, witnessing
what others have only suspected.

Until her step is mellow, measured,
and the pitch of her voice takes on the beauty
of the basso notes of a cello.

When her face wrinkles warmly at your impertinent question
and she tells you a tale of wonder almost too magical for your ears,
this is a woman who knows what she was born to do.

A woman living to a ripe old age.

Leaning into the Sun

Like the smooth-skinned arbutus
leaning its limbs toward the sun

I lean my silver head
against yours, lift

my twiggy branches up to your face
to catch your light.

Crickets

tireless crooners
serenade us
this hot summer
night

my body
young
again
in your arms

Grocery Shopping

Perhaps it was the way I held the ripe banana
or the manner in which he fondled the peach

or the watermelon sliced in half
spilling its secrets.

Something propelled us to hustle
back from the grocery store

abandon paper sacks on the doorstep
tumble onto the kitchen floor laughing

only to surface much later
for melted ice cream.

Pollen

Bumblebees buzz, I just found out
at a very specific frequency
to shake the pollen off the flower.
It's the vibration does the trick.

Just like that honey-voiced man
buzzing at the perfect pulse
so I couldn't help but
shake off my flowered dress.

I still wear the dress on occasion
but this old body stopped
making pollen years ago.

Memories

They slip away
bit by bit
like snow
under January rain,
your footsteps on the stairs
to this empty house.

Blue

There are only a few things I'll miss.

The smiles and songs of the people I love,
the cedars and the pines,
my fig and apple trees,
the chatter of chickadees and kinglets—
the birdsong that begins my morning.
Sleeping Woman Mountain
overlooking the sea.
I guess that's a lot.

Especially will I miss blue.

I read about a Swiss scientist who
invented a device to measure
the blueness of the sky.

Oh, why measure!
Indigo Blue, China Blue, Prussian Blue,
Lapis Lazuli, Flax and Dior Blue,
Cornflower, Cobalt, Teal, Pacific, Robin's Egg Blue,
Periwinkle, Wedgewood and Baby Blue,
Aquamarine and the Wild Blue Yonder.

Most of all, the turquoise blue dress
we bought in Puerto Vallarta
and how it caught the light in your blue blue eyes.

Memory Keeper

(for Paul)

a few months shy of ninety
mind and body still sturdy

he serves as the shared keeper
of my memories

what a precious thing he holds for me
tiny beads of remembrance

strung lovingly together
a living rosary

Too Much of a Good Thing

I was born with an extra lung.
The gods must have decided
this one's gonna be a singer.

Three lungs but only two any good for singing, really.
The extra one, unable to breathe,
a spongy instrument of blood and passion, kept getting sick.

You need to remove something like that and they did.
Half of the good left lung too, just to be on the safe side.
Tossed the whole thing into the trash

with the hospital sweepings.
Never asked me if I wanted to keep it
in the same drawer with wisps of my childhood hair.

I saw a picture of lungs in a medical book:
they look like angel wings
surrounding and protecting the heart.

My wing got clipped.
My heart got a good glimpse of the world.
Maybe that's why I sing the blues.

Magic

When I was a child, winged angels hovered over me
as I crossed the busy street.
A slim piece of bread became the body of my Saviour
as it melted on my tongue.
Saints ascended into heaven after they died.
You could pray to them for favours.

Most magical of all,
a needle scratching a black circle of vinyl
filled my living room with the sensuous vibrato
of a French woman, whispering
the wild romantic encounters of a man and a woman
engaged in *la vie en rose*.

Today, white petalled flowers welcome me into the garden,
opening their eyes to the sun, closing them at night,
oblivious to the stars.
My breakfast, a gift of bread from Mother Earth.

My ripening body falling more deeply in love with rosemary, lavender,
sycamore leaves, the swish of bluegrass under my feet.
Accompanied by the spiralling song of the Swainson's Thrush.

Marie Langis

the only grandmother in my life
she died when I was three

no one explained where she went
what happened to her cozy lap

her crinkled smiling face
her arms lifting me in the air

her hands sewing always sewing
the frayed edges of my gingham dresses
the torn ear of my little grey donkey

like the Little Match Girl
I would strike all my matches at once

to see those soft brown eyes
feel her warm lips on my cheek again

Remembering Tante Pauline

My father's sister, an artist,
arriving in fitted suit and beaver jacket,
crystal jewellery brought from Paris.

Director of *le centre d'art*
in Ste Adèle, a summer school
for the arts in the Laurentians.

Engaged three times,
her tiny feet never
approach the altar.

French, the language spoken
when Pauline visits to sketch
the children's portraits.

Smudging the charcoal on the paper
she tells me I have old eyes.
I feel grown up.

I wear her red shantung dress
with tiny straps to my high school prom
a few years before she dies in her fifties.

What I learned from tante Pauline:
A good life can be flashy and brief.

At the Banff Centre

The music students amble down the hill
to the little Anglican church, hushed, expectant.

From the back of the room, the last surviving
member of the Hungarian String Quartet

shuffles to the altar, a violin clutched
in his hands, all that prevents him from falling.

Bound by divine thread to the violin under his chin,
he lifts the bow, strokes the strings,

his eyes closed in prayer, his body straightening,
he consecrates the room with shades of sorrow,

the wail of the Chinook Wind,
of benevolent gods calling from the mountains.

The genius of Bartok alive in that old fiddler's hands.
I was young then. I would never make music again in the same way.

Remembering Mr. Wetterberg

Rumoured to be in his nineties,
a tall gaunt sliver of a man
enlisted to teach first year opera students
poise and balance on the stage.

He says I'm ready for a match.
I've watched enough Sterling Hayden pirate movies.
I know how to swing a sword, a foil he calls it.
I could kill him!

I don the chest protector,
a mask much too large for my head,
and a glove covering most of my forearm.
I salute my opponent.

En garde! Allez!

I'm in position across from Don Quixote.
I'm tap dancing like Shirley Temple.
I lunge. Thrust! Thrust! Thrust!
His body still, except for the slightest flick of his wrist.
Parry! Parry! Parry!

My foil never touches him.

Arrêt!

What I learned from Mr. Wetterberg:
Age trumps enthusiasm.

Before I Die

I want to learn the secrets
of the mystics, the medicine women,
the crazies and the slightly off-kilter.

I want to write something
I have never thought about
until this very moment.

I want to become a woman
of ambiguous origins and orientation,
wearing flowered skirts and oversized pashmina shawls

sipping rosemary tea in my herb garden,
speaking sagely about the calamities of the past
and those hovering in the heavens.

Remembering Jacques Brel (1929–1978)

With the fury of an abandoned lover,
the rapture of an evangelical preacher, he sang
song after song to break the heart
to wake the heart.

His face framed in tears and sweat,
his hands marking the pendulum of time,
magnifying his pain so we might also feel it,
leaving a scar in the night that would not heal.

What I learned from Jacques Brel:
To sing with the blood rising inside me.

If I Should Write an Anthem for Old Age

It would be soulful
taking riffs from rivers and ravens
who sing the secret language of rain.

It would be wise, recalling
what we learned in our mothers' bodies:
we exist because of others.

It would be short
like the measure of our lives
humble like our frail human presence.

Remembering Paul Baker

Not an old man, yet
nearing the end of his life.

Every morning he arrives,
a new poultice around his throat

to record my songs of hope and despair
in his spacious recording studio with the 9-foot grand piano.

Rescue Joy.
He lives the title of my album.

With patience and skill, he comforts me
as I play through the song

written for my sister
two days after she died.

Ain't life a miracle
Ain't death a miracle
And it's happening every day.

What I learned from Paul Baker:
As long as you do what you love, you're alive.

The Proper Demeanour for an Old Woman?

Just be a saint,
the Tibetan Lama told me.
So I practised my most beneficent smile
my most compassionate gaze
felt my heart swell against my ribs.
But the halo gave me a migraine.

Perhaps angel was more my calling?
I performed random acts of kindness
for the poor and the wealthy alike.
I announced to pregnant women
they were carrying the next messiah.
But no matter how hard I flapped
I could never get those darn wings off the ground.

Might as well just face the facts
I'm gonna be a battle axe.
Sing with Reverend Billy
and the Church of Stop Shopping Choir.
Help Alexandra chase farmed salmon out of the sea.
Stand between chainsaws and ancient cedars.
And keep on raising hell until
Heaven is in sight.

The Piano

She was sitting at the piano, playing
"The Man I Love" when she had the stroke.

The leader of a band in the roaring twenties,
a flapper with bobbed hair.

She kept on with her right hand,
the melody is what counts.

She kept on with "Body and Soul" and "Summertime,"
songs she had played to accompany silent movies.

She kept on with "Embraceable You,"
a song from their courting days.

The baby grand was the centre of the living room,
the centre of her life and mine.

My mother was sitting at the piano
when she died.

Eulalie

My mother's name.
Her American friends, unable to shape
the French vowels, called her Oo-la-la.

Coal black hair and light olive skin
giving her a Mediterranean look,
an exotic in her father's small-town hotel.

Big boned, tall, shapely legs,
curves maintained with the insistence
of a heavy-boned corset.

A woman who gave up playing ragtime
to raise eight children
and a demanding husband.

Fifty years after Eulalie's death
the music of her name—my second name
continues to ululate sorrow and celebration.

Remembering Madge

With her delightful English accent (somewhere
between Buckingham Palace and The Bull's Head)

her bright red lips and saucy air (somewhere
between a rose and the Rose and Crown)

her spicy humour (somewhere
between Monty Python and Mary Tyler Moore)

she brought five children into the world,
loved and fed them all from a cluttered

(to put it nicely) kitchen where
only she could find the bread knife.

Every afternoon precisely at four leaving
the shambles behind to stroll around Green Lake.

What I learned from Madge:
Ignore the mess. Get outside.

The Gift

Her body has shut down.
The nurses have stopped feeding her.

The only nourishment she takes
is from her own body, a shell of bones and skin.

And yet she opened her eyes once,
spoke my name.

And in that moment
she gave me all I needed.

Avoiding the "D" Word

Would you rather "give up the ghost" or "kick the bucket"?
If you're a fan of myth, you might prefer "crossing the Styx."
For gamblers "cash in your chips" and "go to one's reward."

If you're a student you would definitely want to "pass."
Paleontologists could "go the way of the dinosaur"
and gardeners would be "pushing up daisies."

Insomniacs would be grateful to find "eternal sleep"
and miners quite comfortable being "six feet under."
Creationists will of course want to "meet their maker."

As for me, when I realize it's "the final curtain"
time for me to "croak," I'll pause for a moment,
sing my "swan song" and die.

Remembering Marta

Old country woman
rolled her rrr's when she spoke,
Oh I'm so c-r-r-azy wor-r-r-kin'
wor-r-r-kin' all the time.

When she wasn't in the garden
cajoling carrots, snapping at the peas
or hanging her clothes on the line
she was in the kitchen baking bread
or tending to the students
in her three-storey boarding house.

On her hundredth birthday,
she enchanted everyone with her
plaintive Hungarian folk songs.

What I learned from Marta:
Hard work never hurt anyone,
thinking about it did.

Lullaby

He phones every Sunday evening
with news of our large family:
who's pregnant, who's ill, who has a new job.

Tonight he wants to talk about his death.
He's ninety. I listen.
He longs to join my mother.

I offer to sing at his funeral:
the Hail Mary in French.
He has a deep devotion to the Mother of God.

I sing it to him over the phone.
Through tears he begs: *Please put it on tape.*
Put it on tape in case you can't be there.

In my friend's recording studio,
I imagine holding my father in my arms
as I sing this song I learned as a child.

Every night for the next four years,
he presses "play" on his little cassette player,
listens to *Je vous salue Marie* and sleeps.

Remembering Jan

Dapper Norwegian gentleman
retired marine architect

composer of charming doggerel
to honour birthdays and wedding celebrations

cared for his invalid wife for ten years
invited guests to dine on his seafood pie

served on elegant dinnerware on lacy tablecloths
tea poured from a polished silver tea set

never in a rush, time for everyone
in his nineties built wooden kayaks

taught young people how to fence
starred in his own play based loosely on *Hamlet*.

What I learned from Jan:
Set a place for beauty.

The Goodbye

In the sitting room, I touch his shoulders
needing to hold him, afraid to break him.
He holds my hand, his grip still firm.

He's wearing the burgundy jumpsuit
I bought for him at the airport.
He takes an embroidered hankie
from the breast pocket
presses it to his moist eyes.

Such a leave-taking calls for rain,
brooding clouds. Not this brilliant winter sun
radiating the room with possibility.

I recall the day he removed with great fanfare
his Knights of Columbus sword
from its golden scabbard,
the silver blade glinting,
startling my young eyes.

At the door, I turn to wave at this frail man
my father folded awkwardly in a nursing home wheelchair
his eyes pleading with me to stay.

I tell him I love him
I will see him again soon
knowing time is not on our side.

Deathbed Song

(for Helen)

My friend's family gathers around him
in his hospice room.
His daughter phones me long distance:
Papa would like you to sing to him.

I hear laughter, the clinking of glasses,
they have cupboards stuffed with sweets,
art supplies for creating ice paintings,
his current passion.

Not the setting for a dirge.
I reject "Amazing Grace,"
"Tears in Heaven."

I sing a folk song I learned years ago
in the language of his Hungarian childhood:
"Boci Boci Tarka" about a spotted cow with no ears and no tail.

She tells me her father broke into a joyful smile
and she felt her heart burst.

Remembering Gérard

Benevolent dictator
sang nonsense French ditties
after scolding his many children.

Repurposed chocolates, faded
in the sunny pharmacy window,
folded into his Famous Fudge.

Whistled "Embraceable You"
doted on his wife
till the stroke took her away.

Remarried at age 80,
mellowed with the years,
less quick to judge.

At 94, winding down,
fewer possessions,
responsibilities,
needs.

All his earthly belongings held
safe in the nursing home bedside table:
my mother's rosary, her wedding ring,
a collection of rubber bands
with unknown purpose
and a wealthy supply of chocolate.

What I learned from my father:
There are many ways to find sweetness in life.

The Angel of Death

What if dying is not a struggle
with the Grim Reaper armed with a scythe?

What if dying is more like an angel
an elegant angel
in fine Italian leather shoes
tapping you on the shoulder saying:
May I have the last dance?

Sometimes it's a waltz
Sometimes a tango

Sometimes you lead
Sometimes you follow

You keep right on dancing
till the music stops.

Thích Nhất Hạnh (1926–2022)

A cloud never dies, you told us
to comfort those who fear the end,
forgetting the bargain we enter into at birth.

A cloud never dies.
It transforms into rain, ice, snow, tears,
the water in your cup of tea.

Without mud, no lotus flowers, you said.
Make good use of your suffering.
Let it be the compost for your joy.

I look up and see you passing by.
We breathe together.

The Banshee

When you hear a Raven's wing
tapping at the window
you'll know the Banshee is near.

She's come by to keep you company,
to sing you a lullaby and rock you gently
to your everlasting sleep.

You'll hear her whispering
through the long dark night:
Come back home, you've been gone too long.
Your work here is over.

Let her teach you how to walk the sky.
Let her teach you how to dance the sky
and sing the songs that echo through the stars.

The Wake

They tell me it's fashionable these days for dying people
to attend their own wake, not as a corpse, but as a living,
breathing, partying presence.

Seems to me the whole business of dying
means you're no longer in charge of anything.
No more future means no more planning
and after decades of organizing and micro-managing
this comes as a bit of a relief.

I have a short to-do list before my departure:
select some music for the wake:
"The Four Last Songs of Richard Strauss." Grand. Sombre.
Perhaps one of my own songs: "Mitochondria Motel,"
a fond adieu to the friendly bacteria in my body
that have kept me alive all these years
and are now busy with my decomposition.

There'll be flowers, of course, yellow roses, white orchids.
A blues band, perhaps a chorus line of my ex-lovers.

My son, René, will want to serve a good bubbly,
lots of excellent goat cheese, smoked salmon,
shiitake mushroom crepes, and figs stuffed with marzipan
dipped in dark chocolate.

On second thought: Why miss a good party?

Turkey Vultures

I watch their featherless heads
reddened by bloody work

their wings folded
dignified like monks

performing in silence
the ritual purification

of a seal washed up on the shore.
I watch, held speechless by their devotion.

An Important Message from Your Sponsor

If you insist on writing poems about the end of life
seems to me you need to talk about grief
about the end of everything
about the dark furnace of loss, of losing all you had:
the children you birthed, the trees you planted,
the songs you sang, the men you tended,
all of it tossed into the fire with you,
the memories cooked the way your body will be cooked
when they place you in that kiln and dispossess you
of the only thing you could really call your own,
that miracle mesh-up of bacteria cells and human cells,
skin and muscle and bones your parents gave a name to
and that named wonder taking you through misadventure
and mishap always always present to you,
your eyes welcoming the dawn, your mouth swallowing
your morning cup, your hands scribbling the words
fancied by your imagination
your throat warbling the blues
your female flesh embracing the passionate men coming
to give you pleasure, a pleasure matched only
by their going as you gallivant through the beauty and detritus of your life,
the one and only companion of your days and nights
the one reminding you to get to bed
the one telling you when you've had enough to eat, too much to drink
enough crying over spilt sherry and shattered love affairs
that singing dancing slip of a body
taking you home.

Zig-Zag Bridges

My sister Suzanne loved to travel. A retired schoolteacher, she organized her voyages with the same attention to detail as her French lesson plans. Before travelling to Italy, she studied the language for two years, learned how to make profiteroles, filled her library with biographies of Michelangelo and Leonardo, and her stereo with Verdi and Puccini.

She had just booked her flight to Beijing. Preparations for China were even more extensive: four years studying Mandarin, weekly lessons in Chinese calligraphy, and frequent visits to Chinatown for Peking duck and mooncakes. She created an elaborate itinerary of historical monuments and buildings of architectural significance to make the most of every moment.

The diagnosis arrived like a death sentence: *Amyotrophic lateral sclerosis, ALS.*

"Stay home," the doctor told her. "You're in no shape to travel."

Her muscles, already noticeably weak, would continue to atrophy. The beginning of a long, slow, letting-go process, one that would drain her of the life she had known. One teaspoon at a time. Itinerary unknown. Time of arrival unclear.

At first, I dismissed the doctor's advice. I would be Suzanne's guide dog, helping her up the stairs of the great temples. I would be her nurse, reminding her to take her meds.

I put aside my writing projects, left my home on the West Coast, and went to stay with her in Ottawa, the first of many lengthy visits where we shared family secrets, pondered philosophical conundrums and told stupid jokes.

Suzanne was eight years my senior. Because of the age difference, we had not been playmates during my childhood, although I do remember her giving my straight, wispy hair a Toni Home Permanent with cartoonish results. We had had little contact during her eleven years as a nun but, in the years that followed, our ability to be outrageous and silly had brought us close.

The sensuous life was important to Suzanne. She enjoyed a glass of red wine with her Camembert cheese, wore silk underwear and walked for hours in the parks of her beautiful city. All this would soon be a thing of the past. No more boxing lessons at the local gym either. And no more jaunts in her little car, a black Suzuki Swift. She liked things to go swiftly. We would both learn patience.

The idea of taking Suzanne to China was soon crushed. Rather than accompanying her to the Forbidden City, I would be her travelling companion to the hospital Rehab Centre to meet the many specialists assigned to her case. "Rehab" was a comforting word, suggesting she might improve. I took on the role of Recording Secretary:

Elaine, the nurse: *Suzanne's weight—104 lbs. Down from 135.*

Vivien, the ALS consultant: *ALS Support/Education group meets monthly at Collingwood Shopping Centre.*

Joan, the respiratory technician: *Use the breathing bag first thing in the morning and last thing at night to maintain your oxygen level.*

Dr. McKim, the respirologist: *I suspect you may have spasms in the larynx; the vocal cords are not relaxed on inhalation; your larynx should be examined.*

Dr. Buenger, the Physiatrist: *About half of ALS patients have a feeding tube inserted into the stomach for reasons of nutrition, to take medications and fluids.*

Beverley, the social worker: *Live for the day; you're as strong today as you're ever going to be. If you want to move to a nursing home, you need to apply six months in advance.*

We returned from the hospital in a trance. Exhausted by an overload of medical jargon and her prospects for the future, we fell asleep in each other's arms. When Suzanne woke, her voice was strained: "I feel like a Raggedy Ann doll who's lost the stuffing in her neck. I won't go to a nursing home. I want to stay in my apartment."

I assured her the family would rally to honour her request. Her two children, and other family members who lived close by, would schedule visits. I was already planning my next trip. And how we would help Suzanne "live for the day."

At the elevator, I turned to catch a glimpse of the body I called my sister: the crumpled forehead I kissed that morning; the lovely head wobbling on her neck; the hands that could still play the piano but were clumsy at cutting bread; the shoulders small and frail and stooped; the eyes pale, yet full of love. I would take this journey with her.

Back home on the west coast, I played the music Suzanne listened to, so we would both be enjoying the same sensory landscape.

"I turn to music the way I would turn to a good friend," she told me.

The "good friends" on our ALS journey were Gustav Mahler's "Fifth Symphony" and Samuel Barber's "Agnus Dei." I listened, over and over again, as I read the ALS manual, heartbroken, wanting it to be something else, something easier for her.

Because people with ALS usually perform higher mental processes such as reasoning, remembering, understanding, and problem solving, they are aware of their progressive loss of function and may become anxious and depressed.

For my second visit, I was determined to design a substitute tour of China for Suzanne. A friend offered a rare book of Chinese Art, one he had bought in Shanghai. It was a huge book, a collection of delicate pastoral prints of nature and the small part we humans play in it. I thanked him for his generosity, and hauled the book on the ferry, the plane and the taxi to Suzanne's apartment. The book was a hit.

She spent hours admiring the line, the colour, the esthetic, determining the dynasty, the meaning, the context, often in consultation with a friend who was a specialist in things Chinese.

Then we discovered an upcoming slide show and presentation of traditional Chinese Gardens at the National Gallery, where Suzanne had been a volunteer. She got all dressed up, looking very much like the healthy, vital person she used to be, make-up hiding the bruises on her face from her most recent fall, and we set off. First to a Chinese restaurant for a hot pot with garlic and ginger—she could still swallow then, with only occasional bouts of choking.

Off to the National Gallery and a room crowded with people interested in Asian Studies. The presenter explained how these traditional Chinese Gardens had evolved over thousands of years. There were the vast gardens of the Chinese emperors and members of the Imperial Family, as well as the more intimate gardens created by scholars, as an escape from the outside world.

Slide after slide, showed images of luxuriant woods, meandering streams, an artificial lake with a small island, fruit trees, bamboo, rocks and medicinal plants. The bridges were all zig-zag, the paths twisting and turning, so you couldn't see the whole garden at once. You were forced to move from one perspective to another.

In the Scholar's Garden, the central building was usually a library connected by galleries to other pavilions. They were located for optimum viewing of the dawn, the gnarled dwarfed trees, or moonlight on the water.

Most intriguingly, all the halls and pavilions were given names: The Hall of Ten Thousand Volumes, The Hall of Gazing at Pines, The Pavilion of Moon Arriving and Breeze Coming, The Hall of Distant Fragrance, The Who-To-Sit-With Verandah. "The Scholar's Garden," the presenter explained, was "a place to cultivate the mind, a place to meditate, read, write poetry, make music and practise calligraphy, a place to invite guests for tea, supper, discussion and poetry competitions."

On the cab ride home, Suzanne was lively and enthusiastic, even though it was past her bedtime. Except for the poetry competitions, the Scholar's Garden sounded a lot like my sister's "Scholar's Apartment." She had recently left an elegant apartment in downtown Ottawa because she couldn't handle the stairs, and had moved into a rather mundane building on the outskirts to be closer to her daughter. She had brought to her new home the same purpose as the Chinese Scholar's Garden—a place to cultivate the mind.

"How about we name the rooms in your new apartment, Suzie?"

"You're on!"

We began walking through the apartment, carefully noting the view from each room, assessing its purpose, coming up with suitable Scholar Garden names. During the following sleepless nights, Suzanne refined them. She was so pleased with the elevated status of her modest apartment, she insisted I knock on the front door so she could give me the tour:

"You have entered the Hall of Fleeting Moments"—the modest entry hall for hellos and goodbyes. "On your right, for your convenience, we have the Pavilion of Pits and Parts"—one morning she asked if I was going to shower and I answered just pits and parts. "On your left is the Pavilion of Curios and Collectibles"—the storage room transformed into a shrine of family photos, votive candles, and knick-knacks. "As we leave the Hall of Fleeting Moments, we enter the Hall of Gazing upon Poplars"—her bedroom overlooking the poplar trees she loved.

"You will be sleeping in the Abode of Benevolent Beings"—a bedroom for those who came to visit. "As we pass through the Philosopher's Path"—a linen closet reborn as a library with books on philosophy, spirituality, music—"we enter the Hall of Gathering Elegance"—the living room for piano/cello duets with her friend Tomoko, for reading and thoughtful discussion. "And here we are at the Pavilion of Good Eats"—the tiny kitchen where I made her smoothies and easy-to-digest blender soups—"and on your left, we proceed to the Pavilion of Gazing at the Moon"—her small balcony where we sat to observe the sky and the patterns of the clouds.

This was a routine she was to repeat when anyone came to visit—at first standing on her own two legs, then with a walker and later in a wheelchair. Always the same bright welcome to her Scholar's Apartment.

I made more visits, each time witnessing my sister's growing weakness. Nurses and other caregivers came by to offer support.

Soon the apartment began to look more like a hospital, with medical equipment provided by the ALS Society: in her bedroom, the adjustable electric bed that went up and down, in and out, for her comfort and safety; in the bathroom, the Aquatec where she would sit on a seat at the side of the bathtub, press a button and be turned around slowly until she was perched just above the tub. Press another button and she's in the water, much to her delight.

I wrote a silly song to honour this new high-tech status of my very low-tech sister. She requested I sing the song whenever someone came to visit, even the caretaker who came to put a raised seat on the toilet.

Suzanne was now even more dependent on "benevolent beings." More family members came for extended visits and homecare workers attended to her. Not an easy proposition for my sister who valued her autonomy. I wanted to be worthy of this new role. I wanted her to lean on me. I offered her loving, if inexperienced, massage, to help with the muscle cramps and pain. And when she was wakeful, I sang lullabies to help her sleep. I lay awake at night wondering what I was there for, what this dying time is for. It was useless to waste one moment hoping for an easier time. Better to be living the time we were in.

There were so many decisions to be made. One doctor—she had many—suggested she take antispasmodics, which might relax her vocal cords. Unfortunately, one side effect of the drug was the weakening of her already weak leg muscles. When I offered the idea of a Letter Board so she could converse by pointing to letters, she shook her head.

"You'll just have to get used to my croaky voice."

One day, her doctor encouraged her to have a feeding tube installed in her belly, now that she was unable to swallow most foods. It could extend her life a few months. After much thought and discussion, she decided against it. My sister loved everything about eating. The tube would not give her back the life she once enjoyed. It would only prolong a life she was enduring.

Suzanne's priority was to live every day as well as she could. To read, listen to music, visit with family, get her things in order. Each day she found moments worth living for.

The menu was constantly changing as her ability to swallow decreased: from Balderson's Extra Old Cheddar on thin rye crackers, to mashed yams, to—at the very end—frozen orange juice cubes, the sole menu item on my final visit.

Eighteen months after her diagnosis, I received a phone call from Suzanne.

"The doctor tells me I have ten days left," she whispered in the frailest of voices. I was not ready for this.

"What do you say?" I was hoping she would have a different idea about her situation. A more hopeful outlook.

"Imminent."

The next day, I took a flight to Ottawa and arrived at her apartment late in the evening. My older brother and younger sister were already there. They had spent a mostly sleepless night and were going to a motel to get some rest. I looked into Suzanne's room, the Hall of Gazing Upon Poplars. In bed, she barely caused a bulge in the blankets. So small, so pale and—I could see—so ready. I slept in the Abode of Benevolent Beings, listening to her turbulent breathing in the other room, grateful for the presence of the night nurse. She would alert me of any change.

I'd had little experience caring for a dying person. My mother died suddenly from a stroke and my father died of old age thousands of miles away. I was often unsure of my role, how to be with her in this ever-evolving story, how to support her moments of fear and doubt, when to rely on humour, when to be silent and just hold her. I had wanted to make her life as enjoyable as possible. Soon, she would no longer have any need of my care.

The next day, around midnight, the night nurse came into my room. It was time. In the Hall of Gazing Upon Poplars, I held Suzanne's hand and watched her chest moving very slightly.

"Hello, Suzie. I'm here."

She opened her eyes, looked at me, smiled, and closed her eyes again.

She was quite still, except for the occasional rattle of her breathing. Then a sudden deep inhale and an exhale and her journey was over. I felt an unexplained warmth in my chest, as if Suzanne's love was filling the room. I could no longer see her on the zig-zag bridge. She had made it to the other side.

Blessing the Body

The night nurse offers guidance.
I offer song as I place the washing cloth in warm water
and slowly cleanse Suzanne's cooling body.

I wash her hands, graceful in prayer
in the convent many years ago,
hands correcting French essays,
writing irregular verbs on the blackboard.

I wash her face, so much like mine,
slim now, from the illness,
free of worry.

I wash her pilgrim's feet that travelled
to museums, art galleries and architectural digs
and dry them with her favourite towel.

I've been told the sense of hearing is the last to go
so I believe she hears my improvised songs,
my words of gratitude and endearment.

Dear face, you were loved.
Dear hands, you were loved.
Dear feet, you were loved.
Dear belly that birthed two children, you were loved.
Dear bright spirit, you will always be loved.

When we finish washing her body
the way an infant is washed at birth,
we dress her in the multi-coloured caftan
sewn by our older sister.

I have no training in this ritual.
I have not learned the perfect prayers.

When they take Suzanne away
I walk to her living room
sit at her old upright piano
and in the best way I know
say goodbye again. ·

Acknowledgements

With deep love and gratitude for all my dear ones who evoked these poems, especially my sister Suzanne. And to the mountains, cedars, ravens of Bowen Island/Nex̱wlélex̱wm, who continue to teach me how to welcome and engage the end years, with grace, courage and playfulness. It takes a village to raise an elder. I'm grateful to my village.

Thanks to all the early readers/listeners of these poems. Your spontaneous laughter and moist eyes were the encouragement I needed: Paul Fast, Shasta Martinuk, Herb Auerbach, Ann Cowan, Andrea Little, Chris Corrigan, Matthew van der Giessen, Shael Wrinch, Corbin Keep, Erica Thiessen, Soorya Resels, Rabia Wilcox, and my granddaughter, Gillian Hinton; my dear niece, Anne Rochon Ford, who has been a faithful, enthusiastic reader of my writing from the beginning; my Writers Union Monday Muses: Pam Bustin, Diane Bator, Catherine Lang, Kathy Leveille, Alison Lohans, R.P. Macintyre, Philip Moskovitch, Marie Powell and Trudy Romanek; my good friend, Cheryl Genet who, during the editing of my book *Becoming Intimate with the Earth*, persuaded me to include my poems in that prose manuscript, setting me off on a poetic journey and, more recently, for casting a careful eye and loving heart on these poems.

Thanks to all who attended my "Way to Go! Poetry, Music and Conversation on the End of Life" workshops, and responded to my poems with lively, thoughtful discussion.

I owe so much to poet and teacher, Rob Lucas Taylor, for graciously mentoring me through the process of editing these poems, helping me to give them a much-needed scrape and polish, discovering the poem that was truly there. Big hugs to Vici Johnstone, Sarah Corsie and Malaika Aleba at Caitlin Press, for sending these poems out into the world, and doing so with style and care.

Huge thanks to Julya Hajnoczky, gifted artist and friend, who offered me the choice of her magnificent photographs for the cover. I chose mountain avens (*Dryas octopetala*) a lovely eight-petalled plant with white flowers, now going to seed to provide for the next generation. Something I aspire to.

I wish to acknowledge the financial assistance of the Access Copyright Foundation, SK Arts, the Canada Council for the Arts, and The Writers Union of Canada.

"Zig-Zag Bridges" was first published in *Prairie Fire*, Summer 2024, Volume 45, No. 2

"Blessing the Body" was first published in *Quills Canadian Poetry Magazine*, Volume XII

"Handful of Soil" was first published in *Humana Obscura*, Issue 8

About the Author

Pauline Le Bel's writing has appeared in print, on stage, screen, and in concert halls—nationally and internationally—winning an award for her novel, *The Song Spinner*, and two screenplay awards, including an Emmy nomination. She has worked professionally as an actor, singer, writer, in theatre, film and radio, performing leading roles in "Cosi Fan Tutti," "Godspell," "Threepenny Opera," interpreting the songs of Jacques Brel and Édith Piaf, as well as other productions across Canada. She has produced five CDs of her original music, and is the author of four books, most recently *Whale in The Door*, a critically acclaimed history of Howe Sound, published by Caitlin Press.

AUTHOR PHOTO JAMES WILSON

She is the founder and creative director of "Knowing Our Place", a reconciliation initiative on Bowen Island/Nexwlélexwm, unceded traditional territory of the Squamish Nation. In her well-attended Way to Go! workshops, she calls upon her poetry to open hearts and minds for thoughtful conversation on the end of life. Pauline likes to describe herself as an ancestor-in-training. *www.paulinelebel.com*

Also by Pauline Le Bel

Books
Whale in the Door (2017)
They Ask Me Why I Sing So Loud (2017)
Becoming Intimate with the Earth (2013)
The Song Spinner (1994, 2008)

CDs
Deep Fun (2011)
Rescue Joy (2009)
Voices in the Sound (2006)
La tendresse (2004)
Dancing with the Crone (2000)

Essays
"Engaged Cosmology and the Role of the Artist" *The Evolutionary Epic,* Collins Foundation Press.

"Sing Two Songs and Call Me in the Morning" *Science, Wisdom and the Future,* Collins Foundation Press.